I wrote this book as a quick easy guide in a keep it simple stupid format. It Is meant to be a guide to working in the music business successfully. Weather you just want to make a nice living playing full time or take it to the ultimate level of star

Thought for today ..... this is not (directed at anyone person or persons) by the way this is free advice from somebody who is successful and has been in the Music business for over 50 and these are lessons I have learned as of late ... There are very few people I meet that have great talent and all it takes to be a successful artist... and those I have met ... will never do anything out of fear change and risk.... they essentially live in their own little bubble... most people who succeed in the music business take high risks and take NO advice from people who have no knowledge of the music business...When it comes to developing a artist...there enough financial risk to go around for everybody its not just on one person shoulders.... Per one artist it involves at least 10 of 12 people to be in their career....Everyone of these people take financial risk as well as a lots of dedicated time/information/career planning and consulting...it too cost money... before working with anybody in the music business on behalf of their career or yours... these are things you must consider and look for
1. Failure to make decisions 2. Insecure 3.Needs acceptance of family and friends around them 4. Afraid to take any financial risk but wants you too 5. Hi anxiety issues

INTRODUCTION

Although this little black book of music contains actual information that may help career it also is a satire which most musicians will get, maybe find humorous and make them smile.. This little black Book Contains Graphic and foul language with references to drug and alcohol use... So you wanna be a rock star So put your Sunglasses on and read on.

STEP ONE

Do not get a tax ID number not a big deal, you need one, beside you have no intentions on paying your taxes, because gonna live a life of a rock star and do whatever the hell you want anyways

STEP TWO

Make sure you have a name sounds like everybody else. bother to research the US Patent and Businesses Name Dated Base. Forget about doing any Google searches or Social media or even a.com. Just pick a name cool and represents you. Maybe like the Beatles or The Rolling Stones. How about ..(The know it all Motherfuckers) I kind a like it ...got lots of attitude.

STEP THREE

Who needs a web page Forget about having a logo Or getting a trademark After all we are rock stars ...all we need is Face book and You Tube. Any day now going to go buckskin viral.

STEP FOUR

Forget about a bank account Just keep taking cash and splitting it with the band. going to paying taxes anyways. After all not what rock stars do.Oh yeah forget about a domain name who needs one. Waste of time.

STEP FIVE

Just keep playing covers because everybody loves you especially the bar owners. Keep practicing in your barn garage or basement partying and Jamming and Impressing your friends but never get any work done. Oh yeah forget about writing original songs who needs them anyway
Fuck it.

STEP SIX

Make sure you sleep with everybody wife or girlfriend... Get high as much as possible get drunk till your falling down.. Show up late for shows Better yet even show up Party like a rock star.

STEP SEVEN

Tell everyone how great you are...share the joint,,,

STEP EIGHT

Fuck a lawyer ..Who needs one

STEP NINE

Fuck a manager because you guys know everything there is to know already about the music business, because fucking great.

STEP 10

Forget the first 10 steps. And party like a rock star.

STEP ELEVEN

 run your business as a business because really not a business. Never deal with the record company because you trust those fuckers. Make sure you do outrageous and crazy shit on stage ...Like Body surf naked it into the crowd because they love it. Oh yeah make sure you break something, all cool because it gets attention... Especially Your dollar guitar you just bought... You could throw the TV out a window always a winner,maybe even get arrested great headlines self-promotion. LO

STEP TWELVE

pay your bills take care of your family because waiting for your big ship to come in. You need a social media manager. You need any road manager. You need a business or personal manager.You need a producer. You need a publisher. You need a Performing right society.You need to license your songs.You need to copyright your songs. You need a booking agent.You need a publicist.You need a photographer. You need to record original songs .You need a back up job in case your music career goes down the shutter.You need to go to college. You need to musical consultant. You need to run your music career like a business. You need to pay taxes. WHY......? Because when somebody discovers you on You Tube Face book going to give you a e million because of how great you are and take care of That shit... Like have your people call my people man ! Because we are so cool we gotta wear shades.

STEP THIRTEEN

Fuck the original music worry more about your image. No plan for the future just living in the past.Don't worry about doing anything like maybe read a book about The Music Business or go to college. No need to. you going to be a big rock star.Just listen to all your friends and family suck up to you. telling you how great you AR.But not one of them would give you a dime for your career....

STEP FOURTEEN

This is a special day to tell yourself how great you are and toot your own horn, get drunk, get high.just turn the volume up to 11 and jam your ass is off... taking it seriously because everybody thinks great anyways/And forget to play for free as much as possible. Stay up-to-date on all the covers You want to disappoint those fans.

STEP FIFTEEN

The most important thing is never record in a real recording studio, because such a great engineer and producer yourself. you can do it at home...why waste the money, no money means no pot. no drinks. no getting high, Fuck a producer who has been in a business for over 30 years. Who needs his advice an old fuck... And if you do record make sure you record the best covers in the world ... Nobody wants to hear anything new as Courtney would say smile

STEP SIXTEEN

Pawn your equipment at least twice a month so you have enough money to get high you can always borrow somebody shit...Make sure a big fish in a small pond and take any risk playing original material or changing your geographical location

STEP SEVENTEEN

worry about reliable transportation just throw the shit in the back of your car or your buddies car worry about a PA or lighting system who needs it all about your music and how great you are Oh yeah I worry about how you dress non professionally look the better your fans will except you Make sure you play all the free concerts Go to the weekend party Oh make up any CD of your original material because nobody will buy them anyways Make sure one of your fans films you at the free concert and put it on You Tube so go viral and be discovered Keep lying to yourself how great you are and how everybody loves you and gonna be the next big thing

STEP EIGHTEEN

(The numbers game)
Booking agency 15%
Personal business manager 20%
Publisher 50-50
Road manager (salary)
President fan club (free)
(Forgot to include accountant)
Music business attorney an hour or 7%
Accounting depends on who you use

Split among band members usually even ,unless you happen to be a songwriter. Then you keep all the royalties for yourself.
Producer as much is ,000...If he believes in you can work out a deal and he will catch it on the other end.

Photographer usually by the hour you own the negatives
Record companies (stay away from 360 Deals)
Street team Usually free because they believe in the band

A logo -
Trademark usually -
(.com)for one dollar-
Website free to mo.
BI ASAP free

Keep all your receipts for food,gas,Lodging.guitar strings ,new equipment..
Do not take cash....Checks only
Keep track of how much you make.

Run your music career like a Business
Remember people plan to fail they fail to plan!

About the author Jr Garrott

With over 50 years in a Music business he has learned it inside and out... from the bottom up He moved Nashville in early ...Signing with Con-k records. and when that fell through he needed a job any job... Started running sound for local acts in the music community...Driving a coach for a dozen different country stars...Worked as a booking agent for Buddy Lee attractions... The Johnny Massey agency...The Miles Silas agency..Booking the likes of Jerry Lee Lewis,Johnny Paycheck,38 special ,Ricky Skas too many to name...Worked as an A&R representative for Moonshine records, United records.Sun Dial records...he has also work with some great producers Jimmy Johnson,Al Cooper Tony Brown, Don Johnson, Mark Barry,Worked some great writers Guy Hark,Dean Dillon,Bobby Braddock and has written over 300 song release eight albums.. And toured as a singer songwriter for over 40 years..He now owns a recording studio video production company (Artist supporting Artists) lives in New England and Nashville Tennessee

Lightning Source UK Ltd.
Milton Keynes UK
UKHW020713090820
367908UK00011B/631